Introduction

Teddy is Ready! is designed to help protect young pe topics presented in this book are based on current emergency preparedness best practices and standards of care as outlined by FEMA, the Department of Homeland Security and the U.S. Department of Education's Guide for Developing High Quality School Emergency Operations Plans.

Schools are safe, but bad things can and do happen. This book is intended to help parents, teachers and care givers discuss, in an age appropriate manner, proven strategies that will help keep children even safer!

For additional emergency preparedness resources, a teacher's guide and online training please visit www.teddyisready.com and contact your school district and/or local office of emergency management. Together we can help make daycares, schools, and the young people who attend them, even safer!

Stay Safe!

Brad

Copyright and Duplication

ISBN 9781535162494

90000 >

9 781535 162494

Children are great imitators.
So give them something great to imitate.

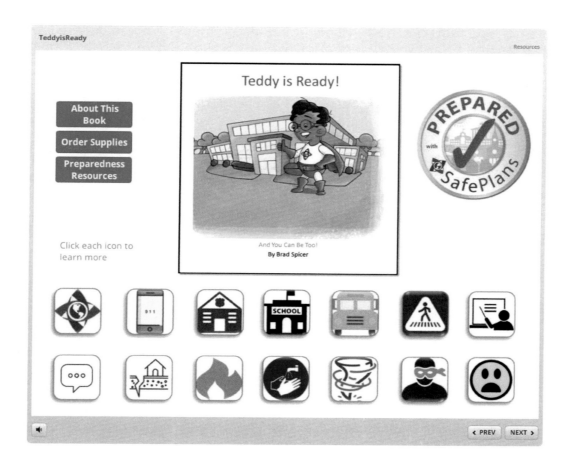

For additional emergency preparedness resources, a free teacher's guide and online training please visit:

www.teddyisready.com

By:
Brad Spicer
Illustrated by:
Sean Williams
Published by:
SafePlans, LLC

ISBN-13: 978-1535162494
Copyright: 2016 SafePlans, LLC

What's Inside

Visit us at www.TeddyisReady.com for e-learning courses
and teaching materials designed to help make young people even safer!

Teddy likes to imagine he is Captain Ready. When a new safety skill is learned, a safety badge icon will appear on the page and Teddy will imagine how Captain Ready would use this new safety skill.

When you earn all of the badges, you will be ready too!

 Be Ready!
 Call 9-1-1
 Police & Fire
 Your School
 Bus Riding
 Walking to School
 Teachers

 Say Something!
 Earthquake
 Fire
 Germs
 Bad People
 Tornado
 Overcome Fear

Are you ready to be ready?
Let's go!

When Teddy was little he sometimes was scared.
Now he is older, and he is prepared!

Preparing is easy and fun for Teddy,
he likes to imagine he's Captain Ready.

To get help fast, dial 9-1-1.
Dial it only for help and never for fun!

Your town has heroes that come very fast.
They are always ready to help you and your class.

Your school has an emergency plan,
to keep you safe the best that they can!

Bus riding is fun, but know what to do.
Before crossing in front, make sure the driver sees you!

If you are a walker, on school days,
use crosswalks and always look both ways.

Emergencies happen, even at school,
so listen to teachers, that's always the rule!

If you see something that causes concern,
say something to a teacher and continue to learn.

Earthquakes shake, so if you are able,
duck under your desk or a good sturdy table!

Fire is a danger so there is an alarm.
Exit safely to prevent any harm!

Cover your cough and wash your hands too, so
you don't get sick with a cold or the flu.

Bad people exist and if there is ever a doubt,
it's ok to run, if you cannot hide out.

17

Tornadoes are windy and blow things around.
Go to shelter and kneel on the ground.

If an emergency happens and gives you a scare,
take a deep breath. That's why you prepare!

Great Job! You Are Ready!

Visit us at www.TeddyisReady.com

The body cannot go
where the mind has not been.

Helping Others

A portion of proceeds from Teddy is Ready will be used to support charities that focus on helping children. Check out TeddyisReady.com/Charities to learn more and track our progress and submit charities you would like considered!

About SafePlans
SafePlans is proud to be the publisher of Teddy is Ready!

SafePlans was founded in 1993 with a straightforward mission: Utilize proven strategies, innovative thinking and the latest technology to protect good people from bad things. From an emergency plan mobile app to on-site consulting services, SafePlans works with organizations large and small to improve emergency readiness. Learn more at www.safeplans.com.

Color Your Captain Ready

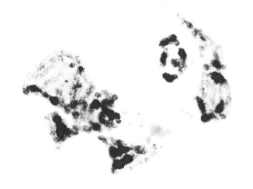

36088325R00017

Made in the USA
San Bernardino, CA
12 July 2016